Look out

at

Home

RED RAINBOWS

The Caterpillar Story
Houses and Homes
Look out at Home
Look out by Water
Look out for Strangers
Look out on the Road
Looking Around
My Senses
Old and New
Sun's Hot, Sea's Cold
What People Do

What's the Weather?
When Dad was Young
When Grandma was Young
My Christian Faith*
Fy Fydd Gristnogol (Welsh edition)*
My Hindu Faith*
My Jewish Faith*
My Muslim Faith*
My Sikh Faith*
My Buddhist Faith*
*Also available as Big Books

EDUCATIONAL AND READING CONSULTANT

Cardy Moxley, Advisory Teacher for Reading and Language,
Hereford and Worcester

Reprinted 2010

SAFETY CONSULTANT

Checked by the Safety Advisor at the Royal Society for the Prevention of
Accidents (RoSPA), RoSPA House, Edgbaston Part, 353 Bristol Road,
Birmingham B5 7ST

Published by Evans Brothers Limited
2A Portman Mansions
Chiltern Street
London W1U 6NR

Printed in Malta by Gutenberg Press Ltd

ISBN 978 0 237 52544 6

ACKNOWLEDGEMENTS
Planned and produced by The Creative Publishing Company
Picture Research by Helena Ramsay
Designed by Ian Winton
Tyesetting by The Image Bureau
© Evans Brothers Limited 1994

For permission to repoduce copyright material the author and publishers
gratefully acknowledge the following:
Norman McBeath: 13; Alex Ramsay: pages 9, 17, 21, 23, 29.

Look out at Home

Helena Ramsay

Illustrated by
Derek Brazell

We must make sure that our house is safe for her.

There are things in every house that can hurt babies and children like you.
You have to be careful.

Never touch the cooker.
You could get burnt.

Never stand too close
to the cooker. You
could be splashed
with boiling water
or very hot oil.

Even grown-ups have to be careful with knives and scissors. It's very easy to cut yourself.

11

Remember, you should never touch the iron. It gets very hot.

Electric sockets are dangerous and you should never touch them.

15

16

Plastic bags are dangerous. Rosie could put one over her head and then she wouldn't be able to breathe.

18

You should never play with matches. It's easy to burn yourself or start a fire.

Never stand or sit too close to the fire. You could get burnt.

22

Never leave anything on the stairs. You could trip over and hurt yourself.

23

24

We must put all of these cleaning liquids out of reach.

Medicines and pills are dangerous, too. You must never touch them.

If you go downstairs too fast
you could fall.

28

Don't let Rosie touch the teapot!

Home is a safe place for us all, as long as we are careful.

29

Here is a room in someone's home. What would you do to make it safe for a young child?

Index

Cleaning liquids **25**

Cooker **6-9**

Electric sockets **14-15**

Fire **19-21**

Iron **12-13**

Knives **10-11**

Matches **18-19**

Plastic bags **16-17**

Scissors **11**

Stairs **22-23**, **27**